THE
PASSION
TRANSLATION

MW00581393

1&2 *Thessalonians, Titus & Philemon*

A GODLY LIFE

Translated from Greek and Aramaic Texts

DR. BRIAN SIMMONS

tPt
BIBLE

BroadStreet
PUBLISHING

1 & 2 Thessalonians, Titus, and Philemon: A Godly Life, The Passion Translation®

Translated from Greek and Aramaic texts by Dr. Brian Simmons

Published by BroadStreet Publishing Group, LLC
Racine, Wisconsin, USA
BroadStreetPublishing.com

© 2017 The Passion Translation®

ISBN-13: 978-1-4245-5484-3 (paperback)
ISBN-13: 978-1-4245-5485-0 (e-book)

Cover design by Garborg Design Works, Inc. | www.garborgdesign.com
Interior typesetting by Katherine Lloyd | www.theDESKonline.com

Printed in the United States of America

17 18 19 20   4 3 2 1

1 Thessalonians

FAITHFULNESS TO CHRIST

Translator's Introduction to 1 Thessalonians

AT A GLANCE

Author: The apostle Paul

Audience: The church of Thessalonica

Date: AD 50–51

Type of Literature: A letter

Major Themes: The gospel and faith, pleasing God, and the future

Outline:

Letter Opening — 1:1
Thanksgiving for Faith — 1:2–10
Ministry Explained, Thanksgiving Renewed — 2:1–3:13
Exhortation to Christian Living — 4:1–5:11
Letter Closing — 5:12–28

ABOUT 1 THESSALONIANS

What a fascinating letter! Full of encouragement and exhortation, 1 Thessalonians will leave you richer in your spiritual life. The apostle Paul brought the gospel to the important city of Thessalonica, with an estimated population of 100,000. Originally named Thermai ("hot springs"), the city was renamed Thessalonica, after Alexander the Great's half sister. The city was home to a Jewish community as well as many cults and false religions.

After leaving Philippi, during his second apostolic journey, Paul and his team arrived at the wealthy city of Thessalonica, the capital of Macedonia. As he preached and taught in the synagogue, many Jews and a large number of God-fearing non-Jews became believers and formed a congregation of Christ-followers.[a] But Paul and his companions had to cut short their stay, for their lives were in danger.

Shortly after leaving the city, Paul sent Timothy back to make sure they were doing well and living faithfully by the truths of the gospel. When Timothy returned, he informed Paul of the great faith, hope, and love that still burned in their hearts. So he wrote them this letter, about two years after the church had been established, in order to comfort and strengthen their hearts. The Thessalonians had let Paul know that they had questions about the appearing of Christ, so Paul addressed that subject in his letter. This was a young church that needed to hear from Paul.

Many scholars have concluded that 1 Thessalonians is one of the earliest known writings of the apostle Paul (along with the books of Galatians and 2 Thessalonians), which makes it perhaps the oldest Christian writing we have. It is dated back to AD 50–51, only twenty years or so after Jesus was crucified and raised from the dead.

In this deeply personal letter, Paul gives us wise and practical advice on how to live our lives with gratitude, grace, and glory. He speaks to the

---

a See Acts 17:4.

recipients as their "father" (2:11) and their "mother" (2:7). Eight times he addresses the Thessalonian believers as his beloved "brothers and sisters." He even describes them as his "crown of joy" (2:19).

Such a treasure is found in the few pages of this letter!

PURPOSE

Writing as a concerned "father" and longing "mother," Paul coauthored this letter with his fellow missionaries Silas and Timothy, to remind these dear believers in Thessalonica of what they had previously taught them and to reinforce what they already knew. After hastily departing them and finding no way to return, Paul dictated this letter to encourage them to maintain their hope in God by persevering, remaining pure, pursuing God's pleasure, and living in a way that prepared them for Christ's return. This concern is captured at the center of this letter:

> "Then your hearts will be strengthened in holiness so that you may be flawless and pure before the face of our God and Father at the appearing of our Lord Jesus with all his holy ones!" (3:13)

Although Paul was encouraged by the Thessalonians' faith, hope, and love, he was still mindful of their vulnerability. So along with his trusted companion Timothy, Paul sent them this letter to build their spiritual muscles, help them live faithfully, and encourage them as they waited for Christ's return.

AUTHOR AND AUDIENCE

There is little doubt that Paul the apostle dictated the contents of the letter that was later sent to the Christian community at Thessalonica. In fact, many New Testament scholars consider it to be not only one of Paul's earliest letters but one of the earliest New Testament books. And yet Paul isn't the only author, for the letter opens with this: "From Paul, Silas, and

Timothy. *We send our greetings to you*, the congregation of believers in Thessalonica" (emphasis added). Paul and his coworkers jointly spoke into the situation faced by their audience, even though the letter was dictated by Paul.

Paul and Silas had a particularly special bond with the Thessalonians, for they had traveled to this Roman city from Philippi during their second missionary journey, after Paul received a vision of a man pleading with them to come.[a] During this evangelistic mission, a large number of God-fearing non-Jews, as well as many pagan idol-worshipers, turned to faith in Jesus Christ. Paul wrote these baby Christians and this infant church to encourage them to persevere, remain pure, and prepare for the coming of the Lord.

MAJOR THEMES

Faith and the Gospel, Explained and Personalized. While 1 Thessalonians isn't an *apologia* for the gospel, like Romans or Galatians, we still discover much about its essence. Paul speaks of it as a power (1:4) and as the Lord's message—a message not derived from the words of men but the very Word of God (2:13), which was entrusted to the apostles (2:4). The gospel results in our being chosen and called by God (1:4, 4:7). The key verses of 1 Thessalonians are 9–10: "You turned to God from idols to serve the true and living God. And now you eagerly expect his Son from heaven—Jesus, the Deliverer, whom he raised from the dead and who rescues us from the coming wrath."

Turning from idolatry and sin, toward God in faith and service, was their response to the gospel message that Paul, Silas, and Timothy preached—the good news that Jesus, our Deliverer, rose from the dead, rescues us from God's wrath, and will one day return from heaven. This is reaffirmed

---

a See Acts 16:9–10.

near the end of the letter: "For God has not destined us to experience wrath, but to possess salvation through our Lord Jesus, the Anointed One. He gave his life for us so that we may share in resurrection life in union with him" (5:9–10). There you have it: God's good news, explained!

One of the more striking aspects of this letter is Paul's commendation of the believers' faith and the outworking of it in love and hope (1:3). He goes so far as to say that because of their faith, they had "become an example for all the believers to follow" (1:7). They had received the gospel "wholeheartedly," not as "a fabrication of men, but as the Word of God" (2:13), resulting in their lives being impacted by the gospel's power. Because of this faith, the Thessalonian believers were persecuted yet remained steadfast (3:7). You get the sense that Paul is inviting us to follow in their steps.

Living to Please God. The theme of living in a way that is worthy of the name "Christian" and in a way that pleases God runs strong through Paul's letters. First Thessalonians is no different. From the start, Paul commends these dear believers for putting their faith into practice (1:3). Yet he goes further, reminding them that as God's holy, set-apart people, they are called to live in a particular way.

First he challenges them "to adopt a lifestyle worthy of God" (2:12). When Paul first evangelized this community, this was part of what he taught them. So he reminds them of these teachings here and makes an appeal: "Keep faithfully growing through our teachings even more and more" (4:1). Why? Because "God's will is for you to be set apart for him in holiness" (4:3).

Finally, he reminds them that they are to live differently because they *are* different: "For you are all children of the light and children of the day. We don't belong to the night neither to darkness" (5:5). While living to please God can be difficult, especially in a culture that lives the exact opposite, it's something we're called to, something God desires from us.

Hopeful Preparation for the day of the Lord. Paul wants us to be prepared in hope for the day when Christ returns in full glory. The main portion of Paul's letter is framed by this sense of waiting for, expecting, and being prepared for Christ's return. Paul praised the Thessalonians for eagerly expecting God's Son from heaven to rescue them (1:10). He exhorted them to be prepared for the day when he does return, keeping themselves completely flawless until his appearing.

In between waiting and keeping, Paul encourages the believers that those who have already passed away have not died in vain but died in hope—for God will bring with Christ those who have died in a declaration of victory!

He also wants them, and us, to "stay alert and clear headed" (5:8) as we wait, for we don't know when it will happen. The Lord's return will come unexpectedly and as a complete surprise (5:2). Yet, though we may have questions about the end, we can be encouraged and encourage one another in the hope that we will "share in resurrection life in union with him" (5:10).

Paul Gives Thanks for the Thessalonians

¹From Paul, Silas,ᵃ and Timothy.ᵇ *We send our greetings* to you, the congregationᶜ of believers in Thessalonica,ᵈ which is in God the Father and the Lord Jesus Christ.ᵉ May God's delightful graceᶠ and peace rest upon you.ᵍ

---

a 1:1 Or "Silvanus," whom most scholars believe is the Silas mentioned as a prophet in the Jerusalem church and Paul's coworker in Macedonia (Acts 15:22–40, 16:19–40, and 17:1–16). The name Silas is the Aramaic form of the Hebrew name Saul. Both Silas and Timothy had been with Paul when he first visited Thessalonica (Acts 17:4, 14). There are only four of Paul's letters in the New Testament in which he does not call himself an apostle (1 and 2 Thessalonians, Philippians, and Philemon), most likely because of the deep relationship he already had with them.

b 1:1 Ministry requires teamwork. Paul saw himself as part of a church-planting team made up of three men with wonderful giftings: Paul, Silas, and Timothy.

c 1:1 The Greek word *ekklēsia* is best translated in this context as "congregation." It means "called-out ones." In Greek culture the *ekklēsia* were members of society who were given the duties of legislating on behalf of a city, similar to a city council. They were both "called out" and "called together" to function as those who have the responsibilities of shaping societal norms and the morality of culture.

d 1:1 Thessalonica was the largest city in Macedonia and may have had a population of 200,000 when Paul wrote this letter.

e 1:1 The church is both "in" God the Father and "in" Jesus Christ. The Trinity is making room for the bride.

f 1:1 The usage of *charis* (grace) in ancient classical Greek carries the connotation of something that awakens joy and pleasure. The Greek concept of grace imparts delight, often attached to a strong emotional element. Paul uses the term *grace* as a joyous delight that rests upon the people of God (Thomas F. Torrance, *The Doctrine of Grace in the Apostolic Fathers*, 1–2).

g 1:1 Some manuscripts add "from God our Father and the Lord Jesus Christ."

[2]We are grateful to God for your lives[a] and we always pray for you. [3]For we remember before our God and Father how you put your faith into practice, how your love motivates you to serve others, and how unrelenting is your hope-filled patience in our Lord Jesus Christ.[b]

[4]Dear brothers and sisters,[c] you are dearly loved by God and we know that he has chosen you *to be his very own*.[d] [5]For our gospel came to you not merely in the form of words but in mighty power infused with the Holy Spirit and deep conviction.[e] Surely you remember how we lived our lives transparently before you to encourage you.[f]

[6]And you became followers[g] of my example and the Lord's when you received the word with the joy of the Holy Spirit, even though it resulted

---

a 1:2 Starting with verse 2 Paul begins one long and complicated Greek sentence that ends with verse 10.

b 1:3 Paul mentions the three invaluable qualities of a believer's life: faith, love, and hope. The Thessalonians put their faith into practice by turning away from all that was false (v. 9). They demonstrated their motive of love by serving God and others (v. 9). And they lived with undying hope that was centered upon the future appearing of Christ (v. 10).

c 1:4 Although the Greek uses the term "brothers" (*adelphoi*), it is intended to express the group identity of those who follow Christ and not meant to be gender exclusive. Paul uses the term eighteen times in five chapters. First Thessalonians could be called Paul's friendliest letter. He describes himself as a "father" and "mother" to them (2:7, 11) and calls them his "joy" and "crown" (2:19).

d 1:4 The perfect tense of the verb implies that God loved them in the past and continues to love them in the same way.

e 1:5 True gospel ministry will be expressed by the word of God and characterized by mighty power, releasing the unmistakable presence of the Holy Spirit, and through sincere conviction of truth will be found in those who present it.

f 1:5 Or "for your sakes (benefit)."

g 1:6 Or "imitators."

in tremendous trials and persecution.[a] [7]Now you have become an example for all the believers to follow throughout the provinces of Greece.[b]

[8]The message of the Lord has sounded out from you not only in Greece, but its echo has been heard in every place where people are hearing about your strong faith. We don't need to brag on you, [9]for everyone tells the story of the kind of welcome you showed us when we first came to you. And everyone knows how *wonderfully* you turned to God from idols to serve the true and living God. [10]And now you eagerly expect his Son from heaven—Jesus, *the Deliverer*, whom he raised from the dead and who rescues us from the coming wrath.[c]

---

a 1:6 True conversion delivers us from many things, but is not an assurance that we will never face painful trials or persecution for our faith.

b 1:7 Or "Macedonia and Achaia." Greece was divided into two provinces: the northern region known as Macedonia and the southern one, Achaia. Thessalonica was located in Macedonia and Corinth, where Paul wrote this letter, and was the leading city of Achaia. Although the believers of Thessalonica were novices, their testimony had spread throughout the region.

c 1:10 The gospel of power will change lives. The Thessalonians had renounced the worship of false gods and turned wholeheartedly to the true God and become faithful servants. Every time true conversion (repentance) takes place, a life is changed. The Thessalonians were famous for these four things: 1) They turned wholeheartedly to God. 2) They abandoned worshipping false gods (idols). 3) They became passionate servants of Christ. 4) They were eagerly anticipating the heavenly Son, Jesus.

Two

Godly Character of Jesus' Servants

[1]My dear brothers and sisters, it's obvious that our ministry among you has proven to be fruitful.[a] [2]And though we had already suffered greatly in Philippi, where we were shamefully mistreated,[b] we were emboldened *by faith* in our God to fearlessly preach his wonderful gospel to you in spite of incredible opposition.

[3]Our coming alongside you to encourage you was not out of some delusion, or impure motive, or an intention to mislead you, [4]but we have been approved by God to be those who preach the gospel. *So our motivation* to preach is not pleasing people but pleasing God, who *thoroughly* examines our hearts. [5]God is our witness *that when we came to encourage you,* we never once used cunning compliments as a pretext for greed, [6]nor did we crave the praises of men, whether you or others.[c] [7]Even though we could have imposed upon you our demands as apostles of Christ,[d] instead we showed you kindness and were gentle among you.[e] We cared for you in the same way a nursing mother cares for her own children. [8]With a mother's love and affectionate attachment to you, we

---

a 2:1 Or "Our coming to you has not been in vain (empty)." See Acts 17:1–9.

b 2:2 Paul and Silas had been beaten and imprisoned in Philippi. See Acts 16:11–17:1.

c 2:6 Paul never watered down his message in preaching the gospel. His fearless courage serves as an example to us today to keep our message uncompromising.

d 2:7 The Aramaic is "Although we could have been honored as apostles of the Messiah." See also 1 Corinthians 9:1–18 and Philemon 8.

e 2:7 Some reliable manuscripts have "We became like little children (infants) among you."

were very happy to share with you not only the gospel of God but also our lives—because you had become so dear to us.[a]

[9]Beloved brothers and sisters, surely you remember how hard we labored among you. We worked night and day so that we would not become a burden to you while we preached the wonderful gospel of God. [10]With God as our witness you saw how we lived among you—in holiness, in godly relationships,[b] and without fault. [11]And you know how *affectionately* we treated each one of you, like a loving father cares for his own children. [12]We comforted and encouraged you and challenged you to adopt a lifestyle worthy of God, who invites you into his kingdom and glory.[c]

The Faithfulness of the Thessalonians

[13]This is why we continually thank God *for your lives*, because you received our message *wholeheartedly*. You embraced it not as the fabrication of men but as the word of God. And the word continues to be an energizing force in you who believe.

[14]*My dear* brothers and sisters, the same thing happened to you as happened to God's churches in Christ Jesus that are in Judea. For you received the same kind of mistreatment from your fellow countrymen as they did from theirs, the Jews [15]who killed both the Lord Jesus and the prophets and ran us out of town. They are offending God and hostile to

---

a 2:8 Or "You had become our beloved." Just a few months before, the Thessalonians were complete strangers to Paul. Now he states how dear they had become to his heart. True ministry is caring for others with a father's love and a mother's love—not exerting control or abusive authority over those whom we serve.

b 2:10 Or "righteousness." The Hebraic concept of righteousness extends toward our relationships and how we treat others. Paul stated that he lived in holiness toward God and purity in this relationships with others, so that no one could blame him for wrongdoing.

c 2:12 Our calling is a summons from God to enter into his glory. A possible hendiadys, "his own glorious kingdom."

everyone else [16]by hindering us from speaking to the unbelievers[a] so that they might be saved. By so doing they are constantly filling up to the brim the measure of their guilt,[b] and punishment[c] has come upon them at last![d]

Paul's Concern for the Thessalonians

[17]Beloved friends, we may have been torn away[e] from you physically for a season, but never in our hearts. For we have had intense longings and have endeavored to come and see in your faces the reflection of this great love.[f] [18]We *miss you badly,* and I personally wanted to come to you, trying again and again, but our adversary,[g] Satan, blocked our way. [19]For what will be our *confident* hope, our *exhilarating* joy, or our *wonderful* trophy[h] that we will boast in before our Lord Jesus at his appearing?[i] It is you! Yes, you are our glorious *pride and* joy![j]

---

a 2:16 Or "the Gentiles."

b 2:16 That is, they are filling up to the limit of their sins before God.

c 2:16 Or "wrath," a metonymy for the punishment resulting from their sins.

d 2:16 Or "completely (to a full extent)." This could be a prophetic word from Paul regarding the soon destruction of Jerusalem in the Roman war of AD 67–70. Paul is not referring to all Jews, for many had become converts and made up the early church. God rejected the empty rituals of Judaism but not the Jewish people. See Romans 9–11.

e 2:17 Or "We have been (like) orphans."

f 2:17 As translated from the Aramaic. How poetic are the Semitic languages!

g 2:18 The Greek word satanas means "adversary, accuser, opposer," and it is the title for Satan. In some way Satan worked to hinder Paul from returning to Thessalonica, possibly through the Jews who opposed him.

h 2:19 Or "crown of boasting."

i 2:19 This is the Greek word parousia, which can be translated "coming" or "appearing." Paul uses it six times in his letters to the Thessalonians (3:13; 4:15; 5:23; 2 Thessalonians 2:1, 8).

j 2:20 The true reward of ministry is not money or fame but the souls of men and women we can influence for the glory of God.

Three

Timothy's Mission

[1]When we could bear it no longer, we decided that we would remain in Athens [2]and send Timothy *in our place.*[a] He is our beloved brother and coworker with God[b] in preaching the gospel. *We knew* he would strengthen your faith and encourage your hearts [3]so that no one would be shaken by these persecutions, for you know that we are destined for this.[c] [4]In fact, when we were with you we forewarned you: "Suffering and persecution is coming." And so it has happened, as you well know. [5]For this reason, when I could endure it no longer, I sent *our brother* to find out if your faith was still strong, for I was concerned that the tempter[d] had somehow enticed you and our labor would have been in vain.

[6]But now, Timothy has just returned to us and brought us the terrific news of your faith and love. He informed us that you still hold us dear in your hearts and that you long to see us as much as we long to see you. [7]So, our dear brothers and sisters, in the midst of all our distress and difficulties, your steadfastness of faith has greatly encouraged our hearts. [8]We feel alive again as long as we know that you are standing firm in the Lord. [9]How could we ever thank God enough for all the wonderful joy that we feel before our God because of you? [10]Every night and day we sincerely

---

a 3:2 This may have been when Paul sent the letter of 2 Thessalonians with Timothy, which would make it earlier than 1 Thessalonians.

b 3:2 Some manuscripts have "servant of God."

c 3:3 That is, the sufferings of persecution are included in God's destined purpose for those who love God and faithfully follow Christ. See Acts 14:22.

d 3:5 Or "harasser," an obvious title for Satan, our adversary.

and fervently pray that we may see you face-to-face and furnish you with whatever may be lacking in your faith.

[11]Now may our Father God and our precious Lord Jesus[a] guide our steps on a path straight back to you. [12]And may the Lord increase your love until it overflows[b] toward one another and for all people, just as our love overflows toward you. [13]Then your hearts will be strengthened[c] in holiness so that you may be flawless and pure before *the face of* our God and Father at the appearing of our Lord Jesus with all his holy ones.[d] Amen!

Four

Holiness and Love

[1]And now, *beloved* brothers and sisters, since you have been mentored by us with respect to living for God and pleasing him, I appeal to you in the name of the Lord Jesus with this request: keep faithfully growing through our teachings even more and more. [2]For you already know the instructions we've shared with you through the Lord Jesus.

[3]God's will is for you to be set apart for him in holiness and that you keep yourselves *unpolluted* from sexual defilement. [4]Yes, each of you

---

a 3:11 Some manuscripts add "the Anointed One."

b 3:12 Or "May the Lord make you increase and your love super-abound."

c 3:13 The Aramaic can be translated "He will lift up your hearts without contention."

d 3:13 Or "at the coming of the Lord of us, Jesus Christ, with all of the holy myriads of himself."

must guard your sexual purity[a] with holiness and dignity, [5]not yielding to lustful passions like those who don't know God. [6]Never take selfish advantage[b] of a brother or sister in this matter, for we've already told you and solemnly warned you that the Lord is the avenger in all these things. [7]For God's call on our lives is not to a life of *compromise and perversion* but to a life surrounded in holiness. [8]Therefore, whoever rejects this instruction isn't rejecting human authority but God himself, who gives[c] *us his precious gift*—his Spirit of holiness.

Loving Others

[9]There's no need for anyone to say much to you about loving your fellow believers, for God is continually teaching you to unselfishly love one another.[d] [10]Indeed, your love is what you're known for throughout Macedonia. We urge you, beloved ones, to let this unselfish love increase *and flow through you* more and more. [11]Aspire[e] to lead a calm and peaceful life as you mind your own business[f] and earn your living, just as we've taught you. [12]By doing this you will live an honorable life, influencing others and commanding respect of even the unbelievers. Then you'll be in need of nothing and not dependent upon others.[g]

---

a 4:4 Or "Each of you must possess your vessel equipment." Some see the "equipment" as a wife, but in the context it is sexual purity, not marriage, that is in view. The "vessel" is our body, including sexual urges that must be kept pure and holy with self-respect.

b 4:6 Although technically Paul uses a term for a business transaction, it is more likely, due to the context, a warning about cheating others by enticing them to sexual immorality.

c 4:8 This is in the present tense.

d 4:9 This "God-teaching" (Gr. theodidaktos) of divine love came to us through Christ. God taught us to love by his example of giving us his Son.

e 4:11 Or "Make it your driving ambition."

f 4:11 The Aramaic is "Keep your covenants (promises)."

g 4:12 That is, self-supporting (financially).

The Appearing of the Lord

¹³Beloved brothers and sisters, we want you to be quite certain about the truth concerning those who have passed away,^a so that you won't be overwhelmed with grief like many others who have no hope. ¹⁴For if we believe that Jesus died and rose again, we also believe that God will bring with Jesus those who died while believing in him.^b ¹⁵This is the word of the Lord:^c we who are alive *in him* and remain *on earth* when the Lord appears will by no means have an advantage over those who have already died,^d *for both will rise together.*

¹⁶For the Lord himself will appear with the declaration of victory, the shout of an archangel, and the trumpet blast of God. He will descend from the heavenly realm^e and *command* those who are dead in Christ to rise first. ¹⁷Then we who are alive will join them, transported together in

---

a 4:13 Or "about those who have fallen asleep." Paul uses sleep as a euphemism for death.

b 4:14 Or "Through Jesus God will bring with him those who have fallen asleep (died) in Jesus."

c 4:15 This phrase (the word of the Lord) is used in both the Old and New Testament for inspired prophetic speech. See Genesis 15:1, Isaiah 1:10, Jonah 1:1, Luke 22:61, and Acts 11:16, 16:32, and 19:20. It is possible that this was spoken to Paul in his heavenly encounter, for he had never met the Lord Jesus, and what Paul reveals here is not found in any of the gospels.

d 4:15 Or "those who have fallen asleep," a euphemism for death.

e 4:16 Or "The Lord himself will continue habitually descending from heaven within the midst of a declaration of victory, the chief angel's shout, and God's trumpet blast, and the dead in union with Christ will continue raising themselves up first (or one after another)."

clouds[a] to have an encounter[b] with the Lord in the air, and we will be forever joined with the Lord. [18]So encourage one another with these truths.

Five

God's Times and Seasons

[1]Now, beloved brothers and sisters, concerning the question of *God's* precise times and specific seasons,[c] you don't need me to write anything to you. [2]For you already know quite well that the day of the Lord[d] will come unexpectedly and as a complete surprise.[e] [3]For while some are saying, "Finally we have peace and security," sudden destruction will arrive at their doorstep, like labor pains seizing a pregnant woman—and with no chance of escape!

---

a 4:17 There is no definite article before clouds. It is literally "in clouds." Where the identifying article is missing, it often speaks of quality, or it is used as a descriptive term. The Greek word for "cloud" is often used in the Greek classics of a large body of individuals, and it is so used in this symbolic way in Hebrews 12:1–2, speaking of that "great cloud of witnesses" that surrounds us.

b 4:17 The Greek word apantēsis is not a verb (go to meet) but a feminine noun (to meet or have an encounter), and in this context it is the bride of Christ rising to be with Jesus to have an encounter or "(bridal) meeting." This rarely used Greek word is also used in the parable of the ten virgins, referring to the virgins rising up to meet (have a meeting) with the bridegroom. See Matthew 25:1, 6.

c 5:1 That is "the specific intervals of time and the epoch (hinge) periods of time."

d 5:2 See Joel 1:15, 2:1-2; Jeremiah 30:7; Amos 5:18; Zephaniah 1:14-18.

e 5:2 Or "like a thief comes in the night (as unexpected as a home invasion)." See Matthew 24:3-25:46; Mark 13:3-37; Luke 21:5-36; 2 Peter 3:10; Revelation 3:3, 16:15.

⁴But you, beloved brothers and sisters, are not living in the dark, allowing that day to creep up on you like a thief *coming to steal*. ⁵For you are all children of the light and children of the day. We don't belong to the night nor to darkness. ⁶This is why we must not fall asleep, as the rest do, but keep wide awake and clearheaded. ⁷For those who are asleep sleep the night away, and drunkards get drunk at night.[a] ⁸But since we belong to the day, we must stay alert and clearheaded by placing the breastplate of faith and love *over our hearts,* and a helmet of the hope of salvation *over our thoughts.*[b] ⁹For God has not destined us to experience wrath but to possess salvation through our Lord Jesus, the Anointed One. ¹⁰He gave his life for us so that we may share in resurrection life[c] in union with him—whether we're awake or asleep. ¹¹Because of this, encourage the hearts of your fellow believers and support one another, just as you have already been doing.

¹²Dear brothers and sisters, make sure that you show your deep appreciation for those who cherish you and diligently work as ministers among you. For they are your leaders who care for you, teach you, and stand before the Lord on your behalf. ¹³They value you with great love. Because of their service to you, let peace reign among yourselves.[d]

¹⁴We appeal to you, dear brothers and sisters, to instruct those who are

---

a 5:7 See John 3:19-20.

b 5:8 The Aramaic can be translated, "be clearheaded in our vision as we are deployed on the battlefield for faithfulness and love, and set apart with the shield of the hope of everlasting life." See Isaiah 59:17 and Ephesians 6:10-17.

c 5:10 As translated from the Aramaic and implied in the Greek.

d 5:13 Verses 12–13 are translated from the Aramaic. The Greek is "Brothers and sisters, we appeal to you to respect (recognize) those who labor among you and have oversight of your lives in the Lord and admonish you. Show them as much respect as possible with great love because of all they do for you. Be at peace among yourselves." Church leaders deserve our financial support and love because of the work they do for our benefit.

not in their place of battle.ᵃ *Be skilled at* gently encouraging those who feel themselves inadequate.ᵇ *Be faithful* to stand your ground. Help the weak to stand again. Be *quick to* demonstrate patience with everyone. ¹⁵Resist revenge, and make sure that no one pays back evil in place of evil but always pursue doing what is beautiful to one another and to all *the unbelievers.*

¹⁶Let joy be your continual feast.ᶜ ¹⁷Make your life a prayer. ¹⁸And in the midst of everything be always giving thanks, for this is God's perfect plan for you in Christ Jesus.ᵈ

¹⁹Never *restrain or* put out the fire of the Holy Spirit. ²⁰And don't be one who scorns prophecies,ᵉ ²¹but be faithful to examine them by putting them to the test, and afterward hold tightly to what has proven to be right.ᶠ ²²Avoid every appearance of evil.

²³Now, may the God of peace and harmony set you apart, making you completely holy. And may your entire being—spirit, soul, and body— be kept completely flawless in the appearing of our Lord Jesus, the Anointed One. ²⁴The one who calls you by name is trustworthy and will thoroughly complete his work in you.

---

a 5:14 Or "those who are disorderly," or "those who are idle." The Greek word ataktos is often used for troops that are not in battle formation (unarranged).

b 5:14 Or "those who are losing heart (fainthearted)."

c 5:16 The Aramaic is "Be joyous in every season."

d 5:18 Verses 16–18 identify three areas our lives we must focus on: 1) unbounded joy, 2) praying continually, and 3) giving thanks to God no matter happens in our lives. These three virtues combine to form the wonderful expression of Christ's life within us.

e 5:20 There is an implication in the context of verses 19–20 that we put out the Spirit's fire when we scorn prophecy. Prophecy is a valid gift of the Holy Spirit needed by the church today. There is no place in Scripture or in church history that indicates the gift of prophecy has ceased or disappeared. It is an active function of the Holy Spirit in the church around the world. We must not ignore, despise, or scorn any true gift of the Holy Spirit. Putting out the fire of the Holy Spirit (v.19) is connected to scorning the prophetic ministry. We need prophets and prophecy to keep the fire (inspiration) of the Holy Spirit burning in our hearts. See 1 Corinthians 12–14.

f 5:21 The Aramaic is "Regard everything seriously and choose what is best."

[25]Now, beloved ones, pray for us.

[26]Greet every brother and sister with a sacred kiss.

[27]I solemnly[a] plead with you before the Lord to make sure that every holy believer among you has the opportunity to hear this letter read to them.

[28]Grace from our Lord Jesus Christ be with you. Amen!

---

a 5:27 Or "I put you under oath (a serious obligation)."

2 Thessalonians

LIVING IN THE LAST DAYS

Translator's Introduction to 2 Thessalonians

AT A GLANCE

Author: The apostle Paul

Audience: The church of Thessalonica

Date: AD 51

Type of Literature: A letter

Major Themes: Faith, perseverance, justice, Christ's return, laziness, and disunity.

Outline:

Letter Opening – 1:1–2
Thanksgiving and Prayer – 1:2–12
The Day of the Lord – 2:1–17
Idle and Disruptive Believers – 3:1–15
Letter Closing – 3:16–18

ABOUT 2 THESSALONIANS

What will it be like to live in the last days before Jesus appears? What words of encouragement and warning would God want to give us? Paul's second letter to the Thessalonians gives us some answers. With only forty-seven verses, this book is packed with prophetic insight that will strengthen and prepare us for the coming days. Not only does 2 Thessalonians give us information about what is ahead, it is also a map to guide us through anything that might assail us as we approach the grand finale of all time—the appearing of our Lord Jesus Christ with his glorious messengers of fire!

Although we spend our lives watching and waiting for his appearing, we must live every day for his glory. We are to be alert, awake, and filled with his holiness as we draw closer to the fulfillment of the ages.

In this letter we find encouragement for us to stand our ground, be faithful to the end, and always make the message of Christ beautiful by our lives. We must do more than combat evil; we must live for Christ and expect his coming to find us as passionate lovers of God, abandoned to him with all our hearts.

Paul wrote this letter from Corinth around AD 51 (less than a year after writing 1 Thessalonians) to his beloved friends in the city of Thessalonica. They were followers of Jesus who looked to Paul as their apostolic father and were asking him to clarify the events surrounding "the day of the Lord." A faulty understanding of eschatology (the study of the last days) will lead to faulty conduct and even a detachment from our duties in this world. So Paul writes to inspire those who are idle to engage themselves with making a living and presenting the gospel of Christ through the holy example of their changed lives.

We all need the truth of 2 Thessalonians today to keep our lives focused on what is truth as we look to Christ alone to be our strength, no matter how difficult the future may appear. One day we will each be able to personally thank the apostle Paul for writing this inspired letter! May you be blessed as you read 2 Thessalonians.

PURPOSE

Building off of his first letter to the Thessalonian church, which he sent just a year or so prior, Paul gets down to business. It seems the situation had deteriorated in the short time between planting this Christian community along with his coworkers in the gospel and his first letter. So he wrote to encourage them in three main areas: to hold fast to their faith, despite opposition, knowing that God will act on their behalf with promised justice; to live faithfully as they awaited the coming of Jesus in glory; and to confront a group of "busybodies" who were burdening and disrupting the life of the community.

Reading this letter, written to this threatened community, will remind us of the gospel's ultimate outcome—the glorious return of Jesus Christ—while helping us remain worthy of our calling by living our faith with conviction every day.

AUTHOR AND AUDIENCE

Although some have suggested 2 Thessalonians was written pseudonymously (written by someone other than Paul, who used Paul's name as his own), there are striking similarities between Paul's first letter and this one. Both contain an extended thanksgiving and a wish prayer, and both close with a prayer of peace. Although this letter lacks the warmth of 1 Thessalonians, it's clear the author already had a personal relationship with his readers. That makes sense if Paul was writing this as a follow-up letter to members of a community he founded, after a short period of time. Given how urgent the situation had become, Paul would have launched straight into his vital words of encouragement and exhortation.

This infant congregation of former pagans in the heart of the eastern region of the Roman empire was struggling to understand their identity in Christ as well as how to live as God's people in a hostile culture. Knowing they faced a dire situation and confusion about vital issues related to the gospel and Christian discipleship, Paul addressed these dear believers with the care of a spiritual father.

MAJOR THEMES

Perseverance of Faith through Persecution. In his first letter to the Thessalonians, Paul acknowledged the suffering they were experiencing at the hand of a persecuting culture. He didn't want them to be unsettled by their trials, and he worried that might disrupt the gospel work he began among them and destroy their faith. Now he returns to this theme, praising them for their "unwavering faith" and boasting in their "unflinching endurance" (1:4) through all of the persecutions and painful trials they had experienced.

We aren't given specifics, but it seems persecution against these believers had ratcheted up significantly, so Paul wanted to encourage them that it wouldn't be in vain. Their perseverance of faith through persecution stands as a model for all the church, one we are urged to follow in endurance, to be counted "worthy of inheriting the kingdom of God" (1:5).

The Promise of God's Justice. In light of their persecution and trials, Paul wrote to encourage them that God hadn't forgotten about them. He would act on their behalf by judging their persecutors in the person of Jesus Christ (1:5–2:12).

Consider all that God has promised to do on our behalf to put things right: he will trouble our troublers, giving rest to those who are troubled. "He will bring perfect and full justice to those who don't know God and on those who refuse to embrace the gospel of our Lord Jesus" (1:8). The ungodly will suffer eternal destruction as a just penalty for their wicked ways, being banished from the Lord's presence. All believers will be adorned with glory. With this in mind, "live worthy of all that he has invited you to experience" (1:11).

Confusion about Christ's Coming Clarified. One reason Paul had written the believers in his first letter was to bring clarity as to what happens to believers at death and what will happen when Christ returns. Apparently, that letter didn't lessen their confusion! "Don't you remember that when I was with you I went over all these things?" Paul sarcastically writes. Apparently not! Therefore, Paul unveils further revelation-truth about what we should watch for and expect in these last days as we await the coming of our Lord in full glory.

As we wait, we're exhorted to "stand firm with a masterful grip of the teachings" we've been given, an "eternal comfort and a beautiful hope that cannot fail" (3:16).

The Lazy, Unruly, and Undisciplined. One might not expect believers who are lazy and disruptive, undisciplined and unruly, to be called out by Paul in such a short letter, yet they are. There's a reason: they "stray from all that we have taught you" (3:6), becoming a burden to the church. Such people refuse to work—"They're not busy but busybodies" (3:11). The example of diligent, earnest work that Paul and his companions had set, and the teachings he laid out, were lifted up as a model for these believers. Since they themselves didn't sponge off the church, neither should anyone else. Since they worked hard to provide food and lodging for themselves, so should every believer. Paul's rule still stands: "Anyone who does not want to work for a living should go hungry" (3:10).

One

God's Times and Seasons

¹From Paul, Silas,[a] and Timothy.[b] *We send our greetings* to you, the Thessalonian congregation[c] of believers, which is in God our Father and the Lord Jesus Christ.[d] ²May God's delightful grace[e] and peace rest upon you.[f]

³We feel a personal responsibility to continually be thanking God for you, our spiritual family,[g] every time we pray. And we have every reason to do so because your faith is growing marvelously beyond measure. The unselfish love each of you share for one another is increasing and overflowing! ⁴*We point to you as an example of* unwavering faith[h] for all the churches of God. We boast about how you continue to demonstrate unflinching endurance[i] through all the persecutions and painful trials you

---

a 1:1 See the footnote from 1 Thessalonians 1:1.

b 1:1 See the footnote from 1 Thessalonians 1:1.

c 1:1 See the footnote from 1 Thessalonians 1:1.

d 1:1 The church is both "in" God the Father and "in" Jesus Christ. The Trinity is making room for the bride.

e 1:1 The usage of charis (grace) in ancient classical Greek carries the connotation of something that awakens joy and pleasure. The Greek concept of grace imparts delight, often attached to a strong emotional element. Paul uses the term grace as a joyous delight that rests upon the people of God. See Thomas F. Torrance, The Doctrine of Grace in the Apostolic Fathers, 1–2.

f 1:1 Some manuscripts add "from God our Father and the Lord Jesus Christ."

g 1:3 Or "brothers and sisters."

h 1:4 Or "perseverance and faith," a likely hendiadys.

i 1:4 The Aramaic is "your hope," making it their faith, their love, and their hope that Paul lauds them for.

are experiencing.[a] [5]All of this proves that God's judgment is always perfect and is intended to make you worthy of *inheriting* the kingdom of God, which is why you are going through these troubles.

Encouragement of Christ's Appearing

[6]It is right and just for God to trouble your troublers [7]and give rest to the troubled, both to you and to us, at the unveiling[b] of the Lord Jesus from heaven with his messengers of power [8]within a flame of fire. He will bring perfect and full justice to those who don't know God[c] and on those who refuse to embrace the gospel of our Lord Jesus. [9]They will suffer the penalty of eternal destruction, banished from the Lord's presence[d] and from the manifestation of his glorious power.[e] [10]*This will happen* on that day when he outwardly adorns his holy ones with glory,[f] and they will be marveled at among all believers—including you, since in fact, you believed our message.[g]

[11]With this in mind, we constantly pray that our God will empower you to live worthy of all that he has invited you to experience.[h] And we pray that by his power all the pleasures of goodness and all works inspired by faith would fill you completely.[i] [12]By doing this the name of our Lord

---

a 1:4 No matter what difficulty we may pass through, a growing faith in Christ, an increasing love for others, and unwavering hope will be the keys to coming through it victoriously.

b 1:7 Or "uncovering" or "revelation."

c 1:8 Or "inflicting vengeance upon those who do not know God." See Psalm 79:6, Isaiah 66:15, and Jeremiah 10:25.

d 1:9 Or "face."

e 1:9 See Isaiah 2:10, 19, 21.

f 1:10 Or "is glorified in his holy ones."

g 1:10 Or "testimony."

h 1:11 Or "that our God would make you worthy (or considered worthy) of your calling."

i 1:11 This sentence is translated from the Aramaic. The Greek is "By his power he will fulfill your every resolve for goodness and works of faith."

Jesus will be glorified in you, and you will be glorified in him, by the *marvelous* grace of our God and the Lord Jesus Christ.[a]

Two

The Coming of the Lord

[1]Now, regarding the coming[b] of our Lord Jesus Christ and our gathering together to him,[c] we plead with you, beloved friends, [2]not to be easily confused or disturbed in your minds by any kind of spirit, rumor, or letter allegedly from us, claiming that the day of the Lord[d] has already come. [3]Don't let anyone deceive you in any way. Before that day comes the rebellion[e] must occur and the "outlaw"[f]—the destructive son—will be revealed *in his true light*. [4]He is the opposing counterpart who exalts himself over everything that is called "God" or is worshipped[g] and who sits

---

a 1:12 Or "our God and Lord, Jesus Christ."

b 2:1 Or "presence."

c 2:1 The noun form of the Greek word for "gathering together" (episunagoge) is found twice in the New Testament, here and in Hebrews 10:25. It is used as a verb (episunago) in Matthew 23:37 and 24:31.

d 2:2 This is a common term that describes the day of the Lord's judgment. (See Joel 1:15; 2:1-2; Jeremiah 30:7; Amos 5:18; Zephaniah 1:14-18.)

e 2:3 Or "apostasy" or "abandonment (falling away)."

f 2:3 A few manuscripts have "the man who missed the mark" (i.e., Adam), while others have "the person owned by (associated with) lawlessness."

g 2:4 See Daniel 11:36.

enthroned in God's temple[a] and make himself out to be a god.[b] [5]Don't you remember that when I was with you I went over all these things?

[6]Now you are aware of the ruling power[c] so that he may be fully revealed when his time comes. [7]For the mystery of lawlessness[d] is already active, but the one who prevails[e] will do so until he is separated from out of the midst.[f] [8] Then the "outlaw" will be openly revealed, and the Lord will overthrow him by the breath of his mouth[g] and bring him to an end[h] by the dazzling manifestation of his presence.[i]

[9]The presence[j] of the "outlaw" is apparent by the activity of Satan, who uses all kinds of *counterfeit* miracles, signs, spurious wonders, [10]and every form of evil deception in order to deceive those who are perishing because they rejected the love of the truth[k] that would lead them to

---

a 2:4 Some see this prophecy fulfilled in AD 70 during the Roman War, when foreigners came into the temple and desecrated it and declared themselves the true rulers of the Jewish people. Roman emperors were considered to be gods. But the one who sits in God's temple, which was not made with hands, is the sin of man, a sinful nature that is traced back to Adam.

b 2:4 See also Ezekiel 28:2.

c 2:6 An intransitive verb meaning "to rule" or "to hold sway" or "to possess." The Aramaic likewise is "Now you know that which controls." The neuter form of the Greek participle suggests a principle, not a person, which could be referring to the mystery of lawlessness in human hearts (v. 7). However, some see "it" as the god of this world (Satan) or the Roman Empire, which ruled the world in the days of Paul's writings.

d 2:7 Or "the secret power of lawlessness/wickedness."

e 2:7 Or "restrains."

f 2:7 Or "until he is removed."

g 2:8 Figuratively, this is the word spoken from his mouth, the Word of God. See also Revelation 19:15 and 21.

h 2:8 Or "deactivate."

i 2:8 Or "coming."

j 2:9 Or "coming."

k 2:10 Or "did not welcome the love for the truth."

being saved. [11]Because of this, God sends them a powerful delusion[a] that leads them to believe what false. [12]So then all who found their pleasure in unrighteousness and did not believe the truth will be judged.

Chosen for Wholeness

[13]We always have to thank God for you, brothers and sisters, for you are *dearly* loved by the Lord. He proved it by choosing you from the beginning for salvation[b] through the Spirit, who set you apart for holiness, and through your belief in the truth.[c] [14]To this end he handpicked you to salvation through the gospel so that you would have[d] the glory of our Lord Jesus Christ.[e]

[15]So then, dear family, stand firm with a masterful grip of the teachings[f] we gave you, either by word of mouth or by our letter.[g]

[16]Now may the Lord Jesus Christ and our Father God, who loved us and in his wonderful grace gave us eternal comfort and a beautiful hope

---

a 2:11 Or "a (power) working of error." The Aramaic can be translated "God will dispatch to them servants of deception."

b 2:13 Or "He has chosen you as firstfruits (in the harvest) for salvation."

c 2:13 Or "by sanctifying your spirits and convincing you of his truth."

d 2:14 Or "share in" or "possess." This is the Greek word peripoiēsis, which means "an encompassing, a surrounding or encircling." Believers are brought within the perimeter of the glory of God through Jesus Christ. There is nothing in the context to imply it is a future event, but rather a present enjoyment and participation in the glory of the Lord Jesus Christ (John 17:10, 22).

e 2:14 These two verses (13–14) contain some of the most wonderful truths of the New Testament. Read them over again slowly and think about all that God the Father, God the Son, and God the Spirit have done for us (e.g., his eternal love, the drawing work of the Holy Spirit, sanctification or being set apart for holiness, faith in Jesus, and much more). Paul states in verse 14 that the purpose of our salvation is more than being set free from guilt; it is so that we would share in and possess the glory of Christ (John 17:10, 22).

f 2:15 Or "traditions."

g 2:15 The "letter" Paul refers to is likely 1 Thessalonians.

that cannot fail, [17]encourage your hearts and inspire you with strength to always do and speak what is good and beautiful *in his eyes.*[a]

Three

Paul Requests Their Prayers

[1]Finally, dear brothers and sisters, pray for us that the Lord's message will continue to spread rapidly and its glory be recognized everywhere, just as it was with you. [2]And pray that God will rescue us from wicked[b] and evil people, for not everyone believes *the message.* [3]But the Lord Yahweh[c] is always faithful[d] to place you on a firm foundation and guard you from the evil one.[e] [4]We have complete confidence in the Lord concerning you[f] and we are sure that you are doing and will continue to do what we have told you.

---

a 2:17 The Aramaic can be translated "He will comfort your hearts and will stand by all (your) words and by all (your) beautiful deeds." Another possible Aramaic translation of this verse is "He will make your hearts a well of prophecy and he will stand you in every word and in every beautiful deed."

b 3:2 The Greek word *atopos* can also be translated "weird, irrational, absurd, disgusting."

c 3:3 As translated from the Aramaic.

d 3:3 Twelve times in the Bible the Lord is described as faithful. (See Deuteronomy 7:9; Isaiah 49:7; 1 Corinthians 1:9; 10:13; 2 Thessalonians 3:3; Hebrews 10:23; 11:11; 1 Peter 4:19; 1 John 1:9; Revelation 1:5; 3:14; 19:11.)

e 3:3 Or "guard you from evil (the unproductive and sinful ways of the past)."

f 3:4 Or "The Lord gives us confidence in you."

⁵Now may the Lord move your hearts into *a greater understanding of God's pure love for you* and into Christ's steadfast endurance.ᵃ

A Warning about Laziness and Disunity

⁶Beloved brothers and sisters, we instruct you, in the name of our Lord Jesus Christ, to stay away from believers who are unrulyᵇ and who stray from all that we have taught you.ᶜ ⁷For you know very well that you should order your lives after our example, because we were not undisciplined when we were with you. ⁸We didn't sponge off of you, but we worked hard night and day to provide our own food and lodging and not be a burden to any of you. ⁹It wasn't because we don't have the right to be supported,ᵈ but we wanted to provide you an example to follow. ¹⁰For when we were with you we instructed you with these words: "Anyone who does not want to work for a living should go hungry."

¹¹Now, we hear rumors that some of you are being lazyᵉ and neglecting to work—that these people are not busy but busybodies! ¹²So with the authority of the Lord Jesus Christ, we order them to go back to work

---

a 3:5 Or "the faithful endurance of (all things) for Christ." Either translation is grammatically possible as a subjective genitive or an objective genitive. The Aramaic is "the hope of the Messiah."

b 3:6 Or "undisciplined" or "lazy" or "not in battle order" or "not in your duty station." There is an implication that there were believers who refused to work for a living. Paul is implying that the church should not financially support those who refuse to work. Personal responsibility is a common theme in Paul's teachings.

c 3:6 Or "don't live according to the traditions they received from us."

d 3:9 Those who preach the gospel have the right to be supported financially and deserve their wages (1 Corinthians 9:6–18). However, it seems that Paul's custom was to earn his own way when he went into a city for the first time to show the truth of the gospel without mixed motives. His ministry in Thessalonica was somewhat of an anomaly. Because there were believers who were lazy and not working for a living, Paul gave up his right to have financial support from them and chose to work "night and day" to be an example to them.

e 3:11 Or "not showing up for the war (battle)."

in an orderly fashion and exhort them to earn their own living.ᵃ ¹³Brothers and sisters, don't ever grow weary in doing what is right.ᵇ

¹⁴Take special note of anyone who won't obey what we have written and stay away from them, so that they would be ashamed and get turned around.ᶜ ¹⁵Yet don't regard them as enemies, but caution them as fellow believers.

Conclusion

¹⁶Now, may the Lord himself, the Lord of Peace, pour into you his peace in every circumstance and in every possible way. The Lord's *tangible* presence be with you all.ᵈ

¹⁷⁻¹⁸So now, in my own handwriting, I add these words:

Loving greetings to each of you. And may the grace of our Lord Jesus Christ be with you all.

Paul

The above is my signature and the token of authenticity in every letter I write.ᵉ

---

a 3:12 Or "eat their own bread."

b 3:13 Doing right in this context is not growing tired of honest work. The Hebrew word for "work" (avodah) is the same Hebrew word (homonym) for worship. Our work can be a form of worship. Our lives are to be a seamless expression of offering to God all of our activities as things we do with all our might for the glory of God.

c 3:14 The passive Greek verb entropē means "to be turned (around)"; that is, to be changed. This was not punishment but an attempt to draw wayward individuals into repentance and bring them back into restored fellowship with the church.

d 3:16 Paul is longing for the guidance, influence, and power that comes from God's presence to be real to them.

e 3:17-18 See 1 Corinthians 16:21, Colossians 4:18, Galatians 6:11, and Philemon 19. The Aramaic ends with "The end of Paul's second letter to the Thessalonians, written from Laodecia (Pisidian)."

Titus

A GODLY LIFE

Translator's Introduction to Titus

AT A GLANCE

Author: The apostle Paul

Audience: Titus, Paul's "true son"

Date: AD 57, possibly 62–63

Type of Literature: A letter

Major Themes: Salvation, church leadership, and right living.

Outline:

Letter Opening – 1:1–4
Instructions to Titus – 1:5–16
Instructions for Godly Living – 2:1–3:11
Letter Closing – 3:12–15

ABOUT TITUS

Who was this friend of Paul named Titus? He was a Greek convert from Antioch and an apostolic church planter, much like Timothy, his peer. Paul describes him as a "true son." He was likely a convert of Paul's ministry during his visit to Cyprus (1:4). Legend has it that Titus was a poet and a student of Greek philosophy when he had a prophetic dream that led him to study the Word of God and to become a Christ-follower. As God's faithful servant he traveled with Paul on his third missionary journey (2 Corinthians 2:12–13; 7:5–15; 8:6–24). Paul commends him for his love, for his steadfast faith, and for bringing comfort to God's people.

After leaving Timothy in Ephesus, Paul accompanied Titus to Crete and left him there to establish the young church and set things in order. Believers who had been in the upper room had returned to Crete (Acts 2:11) and were in need of guidance and leadership from Titus.

Some say Paul wrote his letter to Titus as early as AD 57 from Nicopolis, prior to writing 2 Timothy. Others posit that he wrote this letter around the same time as he wrote his first letter to another young pastor, Timothy, around 62–63.

Titus is one of three letters commonly known as the Pastoral Epistles, which also include 1 and 2 Timothy. Paul wrote them as an older pastor to his younger colleagues, Timothy and Titus, to encourage their ministries among God's people and to give further instructions to the churches he had planted.

The theme of Titus is that right living will always accompany right doctrine. Good words will flow from a solid understanding of God's Word. In today's culture, it is easy to say that we follow Christ, but our faith in him will be demonstrated by godly living. An understanding of truth will bring a demonstration of purity through our lives. God's saving grace is the same grace that empowers us to live for him.

The book of Titus reminds us that right beliefs should impact every area of our lives: family, relationships, work, and community.

PURPOSE

Like his letters to Timothy, Paul wrote this letter to Titus in order to give him instructions for building churches and raising up leaders. It was to be considered as a church-planting manual, helping this young apostle to establish godly lives and godly churches.

It appears that Paul's first letter to Timothy and this one to Titus were both written around the same time, given the close parallels in addressed themes. From church administration to confronting false teaching to maintaining the purity of personal conduct, Paul offered sage advice and pastoral wisdom to these young ministers. In the case of Titus, Paul wrote more to address basic catechesis relevant to new believers, as well as the kinds of problems expected of a young church in a pagan culture. He also wrote his former companion to ask him to remain in Crete and care for the young church in Paul's absence, as well as to encourage two of Paul's companions accompanying the letter.

AUTHOR AND AUDIENCE

As with the two letters to Timothy, Paul's letter to Titus is a deeply personal one, for it was written from mentor to mentee—from an older, wiser, seasoned pastor to a younger, inexperienced minister. It's a letter between former colleagues on the frontline of missions, as Paul sought to give roots to the work they had started together by nurturing the community of believers through Titus's leadership.

Like Timothy, Paul had left Titus among his own ethnic people to continue the work they had started as a team; in this case, on the Greek island of Crete. As a convert of Paul, his "true son in the faith" (1:4), Titus became a trusted colleague in his gospel work. In fact, many believe the two made a missionary journey to Crete to evangelize the Greek island, occurring after the events of Acts 28 and before writing 2 Timothy, when Paul was imprisoned. As a young pastor stewarding a young church plant, Titus must have viewed Paul's letter as a welcomed breeze inflating the sails of his ministry!

MAJOR THEMES

Faith and Salvation in Jesus Christ. You would expect a letter from one ministry colleague to another to center on the good news of salvation in Christ. And Titus is indeed infused with it! After laboring alongside each other to proclaim the gospel, Paul recognized that their work was unfinished. He wanted Titus "to further the faith of God's chosen ones and lead them to the full knowledge of the truth that leads to godliness" (1:1) by discipling the young church to further the faith of God's chosen ones in their shared salvation.

Part of how Paul emphasized this faith and salvation was by calling on Titus to appoint godly leaders to serve as examples to teach the faith, lead people to salvation, refute false teachings that destroy faith and distract from this salvation, and imitate the practical results of this faith: godly living resulting from salvation.

He also offered a basic catechism, or summary of primary Christian beliefs. He reminded them of the grace manifested in Jesus and the salvation he brought for all. He also reminded them of their previous fallen nature, how they "were easily led astray as slaves to worldly passions and pleasures" and "wasted [their] lives in doing evil" (3:3). And he shared with them a royal "hymn of salvation by grace," which declared the wonders of God's compassion, his overflowing love, and our new birth through our salvation by faith.

Appointing Church Leadership. The work of salvation among God's people and the gospel within culture requires leaders who are of sound character and judgment. As he did with Timothy, Paul instructed Titus to appoint church leaders (elders or overseers) who were blameless, faithful in marriage and with well-behaved children, gentle and patient, and never drunk, violent, or greedy. They were to set an example for the rest of the community of believers in how they should live the truth of the gospel through godly living. They were also to firmly grasp the gospel message taught to them, in order to teach other believers the essential truths of the faith and how to respond to false teaching. This rubric for spirit-anointed leaders still serves as a trusted guide for church leadership.

Right Living for the Sake of the Gospel. Right living (orthopraxy) and right believing (orthodoxy) go hand in hand in Paul's letter to Titus. For when we believe in the gospel, and experience the joys of salvation, how else could we live other than in light of this mercy?

One thing Paul emphasizes, however, is that the gospel's grace actually trains us to live rightly. "This same grace," says Paul, "teaches us how to live each day, as we turn our backs on ungodliness and indulgent lifestyles, and how to live self-controlled, upright, and godly lives in this present age" (2:12). Paul also emphasizes the need for godly men and women within the church to come alongside others to teach them to live rightly.

May our right believing never excuse wrong living. And may our right living be evidence of our right believing.

One

Introduction

¹From Paul, God's willing slave[a] and an apostle of Jesus, the Anointed One, *to Titus.*[b] I'm writing you to further the faith[c] of God's chosen ones and lead them to the full knowledge of the truth that leads to godliness, ²which rests on the hope of eternal life. God, who never lies, has promised us this before time began. ³In his own time he unveiled his word through the preaching *of the gospel,* which was entrusted to me by the command of God our Life Giver.[d]

⁴Titus, you are my true son in the faith we share. May grace and peace descend to you from God the Father and our Savior, the Anointed One, Jesus!

Qualities of Church Leaders

⁵The reason I stationed you in Crete[e] was so that you could set things in order and complete what was left unfinished,[f] and *to raise up and* appoint *church* elders[g] in every city, just as I had instructed you. ⁶Each of them

---

a 1:1 Or "bondservant."

b 1:1 Although the name Titus is not found until verse 4, it is included here to enhance the understanding of Paul's introduction.

c 1:1 Or "according to the faith of God's elect."

d 1:3 As translated from the Aramaic. The Greek is "Savior."

e 1:5 A Greek island in the Aegean Sea. Paul's ship had stopped on the way to Rome at Fair Havens, a small harbor on the southern coast of Crete (Acts 27:7–12).

f 1:5 The unfinished work would be bringing believers into maturity in Christ and raising up godly, qualified leaders who could teach the church and lead it forward.

g 1:5 Or "ordain elders." This is the Greek word presbyteros, which means "senior

must be above reproach, devoted solely to his wife,[a] whose children are believers and not rebellious or out of control. [7]The overseer, since he serves God's household,[b] must be someone of blameless character and not be opinionated or short-tempered. He must not be a drunkard or violent or greedy. [8]Instead he should be one who is known for his hospitality and a lover of goodness.[c] He should be recognized as one who is fair-minded, pure-hearted, and self-controlled. [9]He must have a firm grasp of the trustworthy message that he has been taught. This will enable him to both encourage others with healthy teachings and provide convincing answers to those who oppose his message.

False Teachers

[10]There are many wayward people, smooth talkers, and deceivers—especially the converts from Judaism.[d] [11]They must be silenced[e] because they are disrupting entire families with their corrupt teachings, all for their dishonest greed. [12]A certain one of them, one of their own prophets,[f]

---

leaders." These are church elders who would function as overseers, teachers, and shepherds of God's flock. The same Greek word is used for women in 1 Timothy 5:2. Although generally assumed to be male in the cultural context of that day, there is nothing to indicate that presbyteros is gender exclusive. The church elder is called an overseer (or "bishop") in verse 7, which indicates that both terms speak of the same office and are synonymous.

a 1:6 Or "the husband of one wife" or "married only once."

b 1:7 Or "God's steward."

c 1:8 The Aramaic is "one who nurtures goodness (in others)." We would say, "one who brings out the best in others."

d 1:10 Or "those of the circumcision (group)"; i.e., Jewish converts. Paul is pointing to three types of people who will refute and argue with church leaders: rebels, empty talkers, and deceivers. The leaders (elders) must be faithful to the Scriptures in order to correct them and set them in order.

e 1:11 Or "reined in." The Greek word epistomizo is used for the reins of a horse.

f 1:12 Although the Greek uses the word prophet, it is not used here in the biblical sense of a "prophet" of God, for the author of this proverb was a pagan.

said, "Those Cretans are nothing but liars, worthless beasts, and lazy glut-tons."[a] [13]He certainly knew what he was talking about! For this reason, correct them thoroughly so that their lives will line up with the truths of our faith. [14]Instruct them not to pay any attention to Jewish myths or fol-low the teachings of those who reject the truth.

[15]*It's true that* all is pure to those who have pure hearts, but to the cor-rupt unbelievers nothing is pure. Their minds and consciences are defiled. [16]They claim to know God, but by their actions they deny him. They are disgusting, disobedient, and disqualified from doing anything good.

Two

Character Consistent with Godliness

[1]Your duty is to teach them to embrace a lifestyle that is consistent with sound doctrine. [2]Lead the male elders[b] into disciplined lives full of dig-nity and self-control. Urge them to have a solid faith, generous love, and patient endurance.

[3]Likewise with the female elders,[c] lead them into lives free from gos-sip and drunkenness and to be teachers of beautiful things.[d] [4]This will

---

a 1:12 A quote from the Oracles of Epimendides, a six-century BC poet. The first line
  is quoted from The Hymn of Zeus by Callimachus.
b 2:2 Or "old men."
c 2:3 Or "old women."
d 2:3 As translated from the Aramaic. The Greek is "good things."

enable them to teach the younger women[a] to love their husbands, to love their children, [5]and to be self-controlled and pure, taking care of their household and being devoted to[b] their husbands. By doing these things the word of God will not be discredited.

[6]Likewise, guide the younger men into living disciplined lives *for Christ*.

Be an Example

[7]Above all, set yourself apart as a model of a life nobly lived. With dignity, demonstrate integrity in all that you teach.[c] [8]Bring a clear, wholesome message[d] that cannot be condemned, and then your critics will be embarrassed, with nothing bad to say about us.[e]

[9]Servants[f] are to be supportive of[g] their masters and do what is pleasing in every way. They are not to be argumentative [10]nor steal[h] but prove themselves to be completely loyal and trustworthy. By doing this they will advertise[i] through all that they do the beautiful teachings of God our Savior.

---

a 2:4 Paul is contrasting the "elders" with the "younger (Greek, neos)" and could possibly be referring to those who are newly converted.

b 2:5 Or "supportive of."

c 2:7 Integrity in all that you teach would imply serious study of God's Word and its personal application in our lives, and not teaching impulsively from one's opinion, which only leads to arguments and divisions. This gives someone the right to be heard.

d 2:8 Or "with sound speech."

e 2:8 Paul and Timothy were a team. If one were to err, it would affect the other.

f 2:9 Or "bondservants."

g 2:9 Or "submitted to."

h 2:10 Businesses today lose millions of dollars to employee theft. Believers are to be meticulously honest in the workplace.

i 2:10 Or "adorn (beautify) the doctrine of God."

God's Grace, Our Motivation

[11]God's marvelous grace[a] has manifested *in person,* bringing salvation for everyone.[b] [12]This same grace teaches us how to live each day as we turn our backs on ungodliness and indulgent lifestyles[c] and equips us to live self-controlled, upright, godly lives in this present age.[d] [13]For we continue to look forward to the joyful fulfillment of our hope in the dawning splendor[e] of the glory of our great God and Savior, Jesus, the Anointed One.[f] [14]He sacrificed himself for us that he might purchase our freedom from every lawless deed and to purify for himself a people who are his very own,[g] passionate to do what is beautiful in his eyes.

---

a 2:11 Grace means that because of God's kindness and love, in every moment we meet every condition for being worthy of his love and acceptance by simply being ourselves. Grace is unconditional, unmerited, indescribable favor from God.

b 2:11 That is, grace has revealed a salvation available for everyone. Or "God's marvelous grace has appeared to all, bringing salvation."

c 2:12 The Greek word for "ungodliness" is singular, while the word for "indulgent lifestyles" is plural. This has led some scholars to believe that we are to turn our backs on both the root principle of ungodliness and the specific acts that result from ungodliness.

d 2:12 These three adverbs—"self-controlled," "upright," and "godly"—refer to our behavior: our behavior toward others and toward God.

e 2:13 The Greek word is epiphaneia (epiphany) is a nominalized verb that means "a brightness shining all around." It was through the beautiful appearing of Christ as a baby, which brought a wonderful hope to all the world.

f 2:13 Or "our great God and our Savior, Jesus Christ." Note the four great truths of grace in verses 11–13: 1) Grace is a person—"our Great God and Savior, Jesus Christ." 2) Grace brings salvation for all. 3) Grace educates us on how to live pure lives. 4) Grace brings a hope of the manifestation (appearing) of Christ. This is a hope worth waiting for.

g 2:15 We are a people encircled by God himself. The compound Greek word periousios is translated from "around," as a circle, and the verb "to be." It can mean something surrounded by something. It can be charted by a dot within a circle. As the circle surrounds the dot, so God is around each one of his saints. The circle has the dot all to itself. So God has his very own all to himself. We are unique in that we

15So preach these truths and exhort others to follow them. Be willing to expose sin in order to bring correction with full authority,[a] without being intimidated[b] by anyone.

Three

Believers Conduct in Society

1Remind people to respect[c] their governmental leaders on every level as law-abiding citizens and to be ready to fulfill their civic duty. 2And remind them to never tear down anyone with their words or quarrel,[d] but instead be considerate, humble, and courteous to everyone. 3For it wasn't that long ago that we behaved foolishly in our stubborn disobedience. We were easily led astray as slaves to worldly passions and pleasures. We wasted our lives in doing evil, and with hateful jealousy we hated others.

---

belong only to him. Uniquely his, we are monopolized by God, taken into himself by grace through faith and surrounded by his love.

a 2:15 Or "Speak these things; exhort or rebuke (speak in order to expose sin and bring correction) with all authority."

b 2:15 Or "disregarded."

c 3:1 Or "be subject to."

d 3:2 Or "strive with others." The implication is that we accept the differences of others and allow people to be who they are and not try to make them over into our image of who we think they should be.

The Hymn of Salvation by Grace

[4]When the extraordinary compassion of God our Savior[a]
and his overpowering love suddenly appeared *in person,*
as the brightness of a dawning day,[b]
[5]he came to save us.
Not because of any virtuous deed that we have done
but only because of his extravagant mercy.
[6]He saved us,
resurrecting us[c] through the washing of rebirth.
We are made completely new by the Holy Spirit,[d]
whom he splashed over us richly
by Jesus, the Messiah, our Life Giver.
[7]So as a gift of his love,
and since we are faultless—
innocent before his face—
we can now become heirs *of all things,*
all because of an overflowing hope of eternal life.

[8]How true and faithful is this message!

Faith Produces Good Works

I want you to especially emphasize[e] these truths, so that those who believe in God will be careful to devote themselves to doing good works.

---

a 3:4 Many scholars believe that verses 4–7 are ancient Christian poetry or perhaps the words to a hymn.

b 3:4 Implied in the Greek word epiphainō (epiphany), which means "to shine forth (brightly) in an appearing."

c 3:6 As translated from the Aramaic.

d 3:6 All three members of the Trinity are mentioned in verses 4–6 and are seen as active participants in our salvation.

e 3:8 Or "affirm strongly," an hapax legomenon.

It is *always* beautiful and profitable *for believers* to do good works.

⁹But avoid useless controversies,ᵃ genealogies,ᵇ pointless quarrels, and arguments over the law, which will get you nowhere.ᶜ ¹⁰After a first and second warning, have nothing more to do with a divisive person *who refuses to be corrected.* ¹¹For you know that such a one is entwined with his sin and stands self-condemned.

Paul's Coworkers

¹²When I send Artemasᵈ or Tychicusᵉ to you, be sure to meet me at the City of Victory,ᶠ for I've decided to spend the winter there.

¹³Give a generous send-off to Zenas the scribeᵍ and Apollos,ʰ and send them on their journey with what they need.

---

a 3:9 The Aramaic is "offensive debates."

b 3:9 The Aramaic is "tribal traditions."

c 3:9 See also Hebrews 13:9.

d 3:12 Artemas, or "Artemas of Lystra," was considered to be one of the seventy disciples whom Jesus sent out.

e 3:12 Tychichus, an Ephesian, was a beloved coworker of Paul and is mentioned five times in the New Testament (Acts 20:4; Ephesians 6:21; Colossians 4:7; 2 Timothy 4:12). He was listed among the seventy disciples whom Jesus sent out according to Hippolytus of Rome. See Francis Mershman, "St. Tychicus" (1913) and Charles Herbermann, Catholic Encyclopedia.

f 3:12 Or "Nicopolis," a Greek city on the western shore. Nicopolis means "the City of Victory."

g 3:13 Or "lawyer." The word translated "lawyer" can be used for either Greek or Roman law. Zenas is considered to be one of the seventy whom Jesus sent out.

h 3:13 Apollos was a powerful preacher and coworker of Paul, who was very influential in the church of Corinth. He is listed ten times in the New Testament (Acts 18:24; 19:1; 1 Corinthians 1:12; 3:4–6, 22; 4:6; 16:12). Jerome states that Apollos, after Paul's letters brought healing to the divisions of the church in Corinth, returned and became an elder (overseer) in the church. See Jerome, Commentary on the Epistle of Titus.

Conclusion

[14]Encourage the believers to be passionately devoted to beautiful works of righteousness by meeting the urgent needs of others and not be unfruitful.

[15]Everyone here with me sends their loving greetings to you. Greet the believers who love us in the faith. May God's wonderful grace be with you all!

Love in Christ,

Paul[a]

---

a 3:15 The Aramaic adds, "The end of the letter written by Paul to Titus from Nicopolis, sent by the hand of Zenas and Apollos."

Philemon

FORGIVING LOVE

Translator's Introduction to Philemon

AT A GLANCE

Author: The apostle Paul

Audience: Philemon, a slave owner

Date: AD 60–61

Type of Literature: A letter

Major Themes: Christian love, Christian belonging, fellowship, and slavery.

Outline:

Letter Opening – 1–3
Paul's Appreciation for Philemon – 4–7
Paul's Appeal on Behalf of Onesimus – 8–22
Letter Closing – 23–25

ABOUT PHILEMON

Paul's letter to Philemon is perhaps one of the most fascinating portions of our New Testament. It is a letter written with one purpose—to bring reconciliation between two brothers in Christ. It is a letter that promotes forgiveness as the key to unity and reconciliation. Everyone has experienced being offended, and everyone has offended another person. Yet in Christ, there is enough love to cover all sin and enough forgiveness to reconcile with those who have hurt or wounded us.

Here's the backstory of this intriguing letter: Philemon had been one of Paul's numerous coworkers in ministry. There was much history between Paul and Philemon, a person Paul considered a dear and trusted friend. It is believed that Philemon was wealthy, and along with his wife, led a dynamic house church in the city of Colossae, a city in Asia Minor (modern day Turkey). Although Paul had never visited Colossae[a], there remained a strong bond of friendship between Philemon and Paul.

Apparently, Philemon owned a slave who stole from him and ran away. His name was Onesimus[b]. By events that only God could orchestrate, the fugitive Onesimus found himself imprisoned next to Paul. Through the ministry of the Holy Spirit, Paul led his fellow prisoner to the Lord.

Paul sent the runaway slave back to Philemon carrying this letter in his hand asking his former master to fully receive Onesimus and be restored to him as a fellow believer. A slave who ran away could be punished by death according to the Roman laws of this era, yet Paul not only said Philemon should forgive him, but also love him as a brother returning home. This made-for-a-movie plot is contained in this very short letter you are about to read.

---

a See Colossians 2:1.

b Onesimus means "useful" or "valuable." See Colossians 4:9. This reference of Onesimus in Colossians suggests that Colossians was written shortly after Philemon.

Orthodox Church tradition tells us that Onesimus served Christ faithfully throughout his life and became the bishop of the church of Ephesus after Timothy's death. The slave-turned-bishop was later taken once again as a prisoner to Rome where he testified before his judge Tertylus. He was condemned to death by stoning, and afterwards his corpse was beheaded in AD 109.

We should be grateful to God for gifting us this letter, because the dignity of every human being is brought forth powerfully in the story of Philemon and Onesimus—a story of forgiving love!

PURPOSE

The apostle Paul wrote his friend Philemon, a slave owner, mainly to encourage him to forgive and restore his slave Onesimus—and to do so no longer as a slave but as a brother in Christ. The theme of the book of Philemon is forgiving love. Love forgives, restores, covers sin, and heals broken relationships. The sweetness of reconciliation is an incomparable joy. Only the love of Christ has the power to perform such a glorious restoration of relationships. We can thank God that he has given us this amazing letter to bring hope that forgiveness is waiting—waiting for all of us to experience for ourselves.

AUTHOR AND AUDIENCE

While a prisoner for the sake of the gospel, the apostle Paul wrote to a slave owner named Philemon. Although four names are listed in the letter's opening, it was customary in ancient letters to list the primary addressee first. It is clear throughout the main body of the letter that Paul singled out a single individual in his appeal: Philemon. This letter was a precious piece of correspondence between brothers bound by brotherly and Christian love.

And yet it wasn't entirely private, for two other names and "the church" were also included, revealing the important bond between brothers and sisters in their activities through their common faith in Christ. This letter becomes a window into the heart of God for Christ's community, urging generous forgiving love.

MAJOR THEMES

Christian Belonging in a Common Faith. Mentioning Apphia and Archippus, as well as Philemon's house church, turned what might have been a private conversation into a public appeal. Though Paul may have been seeking to exert some sort of social pressure on Philemon, one of the enduring, relevant teachings of this letter is that our private business is a matter for the believing community since we belong to one another in a common faith.

Paul's use of *koinonia* (Greek for "fellowship") in verse 6 captures this reality. When people commit themselves to Christ, they are also committing themselves to a community. They bind themselves and become identified with one another so that they receive both the benefits and responsibilities of that "belonging." Paul invited Philemon and Onesimus, in addition to the house church, to think through the radical implications of their belonging to one another as slave and master, as well as a believing community.

The Love of Christ Performed. It is clear from Paul's entire work, as well as the general tone of this letter, that his appeal was rooted in the love of Christ. But it isn't only that Paul wanted Philemon to respond to Onesimus in forgiveness and restoration in the same way Christ has responded to us. The manner in which Paul wrote his appeal and advocated for Onesimus—his tone and tenor, his words and arguments—also reflected the tender love of Christ.

We perform the same love which Christ himself performed. Paul performed Christ's love when he advocated for Onesimus, and in the way he appealed to Philemon. And he wanted Philemon to follow his performance with his slave-turned-brother.

Slavery and Brotherhood. There's an obvious facet to the relationship between Philemon and Onesiums: slavery. To our modern ears we think the antebellum South and injustices of the eighteenth and nineteenth centuries. Yet slavery looked quite different in the first century, so Paul wouldn't have necessarily viewed it as sinister, and he didn't seem to offer a treatise on abolitionism in his letter.

Still Paul is clearly interested that "we no longer see each other in our former state—enslaved or free—because we're all one through our union with Jesus Christ with no distinction between us" (Galatians 3:28). He wanted Philemon to reflect this common union in how he treated Onesimus: "welcome him no longer as a slave, but more than that, as a dearly loved brother" (16). Onesimus had gone from being a valuable slave to a valuable brother in Christ (10–11).

This letter, then, seems to be less about slavery and more about the relationship between a slave and his master, now brothers in the Lord who Paul wants to experience forgiving love.

One

—

1-2From Paul, a prisoner[a] of the Anointed One, Jesus, and Timothy our brother, to Philemon,[b] our precious friend and companion in this work, and to the church that meets in his house, along with our dear sister Apphia and our fellow soldier Archippus.[c]

3May God our Father and the Lord Jesus Christ pour out his grace and peace upon you.

Philemon's Faith and Love

4I am always thankful to my God as I remember you in my prayers 5because I'm hearing reports about your faith in the Lord Jesus and how much love you have for all his holy followers. 6I pray for you that the faith we share[d] may effectively deepen your understanding of every

---

a 1–2 In other letters from Paul, he describes himself as an apostle, but here, writing to his dear friend, there is no need to remind Philemon of his apostleship.

b 1-2 Philemon means "affectionate" and is derived from the Greek word philema, which means "kiss."

c 1-2 Apphia means "fruitful one" and is believed to be the name of Philemon's wife. Archippus means "master of the horse" and was possibly their son's name. See also Colossians 4:17.

d 6 This is somewhat ambiguous, for the Greek is literally "for the sharing of the faith of you." It can mean a number of things, including the common faith that Paul and Philemon shared, or it could mean the faith that Philemon shared with others through evangelism. The Aramaic can be translated "May your association (fellowship) of believers (Philemon's house church) be fruitful in works and in the knowledge of all that you possess in Jesus, the Messiah."

good thing that belongs to you in Christ. [7]Your love *has impacted me* and brings me great joy and encouragement, for the hearts of the believers have been greatly refreshed through you, dear brother.

Paul's Request on Behalf of Onesimus

[8]Even though I have enough boldness in Christ that I could command you to do what is proper, [9-10]I'd much rather make an appeal because of our friendship. So here I am, an old man,[a] a prisoner for Christ, making my loving appeal to you. It is on behalf of my child, whose spiritual father I became[b] while here in prison; that is, Onesimus.[c] [11]Formerly he was not useful or valuable to you, but now he is valuable to both of us. [12]He is my very heart,[d] and I've sent him back to you *with this letter*.

[13]I would have preferred to keep him at my side so that he could take your place as my helper during my imprisonment for the sake of the gospel.[e] [14]However, I did not want to make this decision without your consent, so that your act of kindness[f] would not be a matter of obligation but out of willingness.

[15]Perhaps *you could think of it this way*: he was separated from you for a short time so that you could have him back forever. [16]So welcome

---

a 9 Some manuscripts have "an ambassador" in place of "an old man."

b 10 The Aramaic is "whom I birthed with my chains (while in prison)."

c 8 Paul employs a masterful play on words, for the name Onesimus means "useful" or "valuable." The book of Philemon is a masterpiece of grace, tact, and love.

d 12 The Aramaic is "for he is my son." It would be hard to imagine a more powerful way to describe the affection between Paul and his spiritual son, Onesimus. The one who gave us the love chapter (1 Corinthians 13) demonstrated that love in his relationships, even with those who were much younger than he.

e 13 Or "in the chains of the gospel." The Aramaic changes the object of the phrase to Onesimus: "I took him to serve me, chained to God's message, on your behalf."

f 14 By implication, this act of kindness refers to Philemon receiving the fugitive slave back with love and forgiveness.

him no longer as a slave, but more than that, as a dearly loved brother. He is that to me especially, and how much more so to you, both humanly speaking and in the Lord.

¹⁷So if you consider me your friend and partner, accept him the same way you would accept me. ¹⁸And if he has stolen anything[a] from you or owes you anything, just place it on my account.

¹⁹I, Paul, have written these words in my own handwriting. I promise to pay you back everything, to say nothing of the fact that you owe me your very self.[b]

²⁰Yes, my brother, enrich my soul[c] in the Lord—refresh my heart in Christ! ²¹I'm writing to you with confidence that you will comply with my request and do even more than what I'm asking.

²²And would you do one more thing for me? Since I'm hoping through your prayers to be restored to you soon, please prepare a guest room for me.

²³Epaphras, my fellow prisoner in the Anointed One, Jesus, sends his

---

a 18 Although the Greek verb adikeō means "to do wrong" or "to defraud," the clear implication is that Onesimus had stolen from his master.

b 19 By implication, it was Paul who had brought the message of life to Philemon and became his "spiritual father" as well.

c 20 Or "benefited" or "profited." This is a play on words that would not be lost on the educated Philemon, for it is taken from the root word for Onesimus (profitable).

greetings of peace[a] to you, [24]and so does Mark,[b] Aristarchus,[c] Demas,[d] and Luke, my companions in this ministry.

[25]May the unconditional love[e] of the Lord Jesus, the Anointed One, be with your spirit![f]

---

a 23 The cultural greeting of that day would be peace or "shalom."

b 24 That is, "John Mark." See Acts 15:36–40. This shows that John Mark was fully restored in his relationship and partnership with the apostle Paul. Since Mark's death was in Alexandria in AD 62, the book of Philemon was obviously written before then. This is the only place in the New Testament that records Mark and Luke being in the same place. Paul had two gospel writers who traveled with him.

c 24 Aristarchus means "best prince (ruler)." He was also known as Aristarchus of Thessalonica and is identified in church history as one of the seventy whom Jesus sent out. He was both a ministry companion of Paul and Paul's "fellow prisoner" (Colossians 4:10).

d 24 Demas means "governor of the people." Demas would later desert Paul and turn back to the world. See 2 Timothy 4:10.

e 25 Or "grace."

f 25 The Aramaic adds a postscript: "End of the letter of Philemon, which was written from Rome and sent by the hands of Onesimus."

About The Passion Translation

The message of God's story is timeless; the Word of God doesn't change. But the methods by which that story is communicated should be timely; the vessels that steward God's Word can and should change.

One of those timely methods and vessels is Bible translations. Bible translations are both a gift and a problem. They give us the words God spoke through his servants, but words can be very poor containers for revelation because they leak! The meanings of words change from one generation to the next. Meaning is influenced by culture, background, and many other details. You can imagine how differently the Hebrew authors of the Old Testament saw the world three thousand years ago from the way we see it today!

There is no such thing as a truly literal translation of the Bible, for there is not an equivalent language that perfectly conveys the meaning of the biblical text except as it is understood in its original cultural and linguistic setting. This problem is best addressed when we seek to transfer meaning, not merely words, from the original text to the receptor language.

The purpose of *The Passion Translation* is to reintroduce the passion and fire of the Bible to the English reader. It doesn't merely convey the original, literal meaning of words. It expresses God's passion for people and his world by translating the original, life-changing message of God's Word for modern readers.

You will notice at times we've italicized certain words or phrases. These highlighted portions are not in the original Hebrew, Greek, or Aramaic manuscripts but are implied from the context. We've made these implications explicit for the sake of narrative clarity and to better convey the meaning of God's Word. This is a common practice by mainstream translations, including the New American Standard Bible and the King James Version.

We've also chosen to translate certain names in their original Hebrew or Greek form to better convey their cultural meaning and significance. For instance, translations of the Bible have substituted Jacob with James. Both Greek and Aramaic leave this Hebrew name in its original form. Therefore, this translation uses the correct cultural name.

God longs to have his Word expressed in every language in a way that would unlock the passion of his heart. Our goal is to trigger inside every English–speaking reader an overwhelming response to the truth of the Bible. This is a heart-level translation, from the passion of God's heart to the passion of your heart.

We pray this version of God's Word will kindle in you a burning desire for him and his heart, while impacting the church for years to come.

About the Translator

Dr. Brian Simmons is known as a passionate lover of God. After a dramatic conversion to Christ, Brian knew that God was calling him to go to the unreached people of the world and present the gospel of God's grace to all who would listen. With his wife, Candice, and their three children, he spent nearly eight years in the tropical rain forest of the Darien Province of Panama as a church planter, translator, and consultant. Brian was involved in the Paya-Kuna New Testament translation project. He studied linguistics and Bible translation principles with New Tribes Mission. After their ministry in the jungle, Brian was instrumental in planting a thriving church in New England (USA), and now travels full time as a speaker and Bible teacher. He has been happily married to Candice for over forty-two years and is known to boast regularly of his children and grandchildren. Brian and Candice may be contacted at:

Facebook.com/passiontranslation
Twitter.com/tPtBible

For more information about the translation project or any of Brian's books, please visit:

thePassionTranslation.com
StairwayMinistries.org

thepassiontranslation.com